# Praise for *Attic Rain*....

"I could say you'll return again and again to *Attic Rain* because in these poems Samantha Jones returns again and again to check that everything is ok. I won't but if I did, it would reflect her deft wit and formal inventiveness. She writes with a lightness which belies the implicit pain of the experience of OCD. With self-awareness, energy and agency, she transforms anxiety-motivated repetition into the music of poetry and creates quirky diagrams which map the difficult routes of her OCD with insight. This is a book that isn't afraid to record and appreciate the strange, challenging and absurd delight of being human."

—**GARY BARWIN** award-winning author of *Scandal at the Alphorn Factory*

"Never have I read a poetry collection quite like this! *Attic Rain* is artful, intimate and original in its exploration of OCD. Each poem and illustration offers the reader palpable panic and delight."

—**FARZANA DOCTOR,** award-winning author of *The Beauty of Us*

"Samantha Jones speaks with a strong new voice in these poems about her lived experience of neurodivergence, obsessive-compulsive disorder, and climate change, and the impact of a shifting world on all who rely on stability and patterns to retain a crucial feeling of safety. Self-reflective, wry, intelligent, and vulnerable, *Attic Rain* is a brave debut collection from a brilliant writer to watch."

—**JENNA BUTLER,** award-winning author of *Revery: A Year of Bees*

"*Attic Rain* is a raw poetic map, a song of compulsion, a charting of what it means to live in and see the world as someone called upon to check and then check again. If Psychiatry's single greatest reference point, the DSM 5 Handbook, could have a heart, it would be *Attic Rain*. If Faculties of Medicine ever wanted to teach truly patient-centred caring, they'd use *Attic Rain* as a textbook. *Attic Rain* demands second looks, double and triple trips: this is poetry that wears thin a path in your carpet as you trace and retrace all the book has to offer."

—**SARAH DE LEEUW,** award-winning author of *Geographies of a Lover*

ATTIC RAIN

# ATTIC

# RAIN

POEMS

SAMANTHA JONES

Copyright © 2024 Samantha Jones

All rights reserved. The use of any part of this publication reproduced, transmitted in any form or by any means, electronic, mechanical, recording or otherwise, or stored in a retrieval system, without the prior consent of the publisher is an infringement of the copyright law. In the case of photocopying or other reprographic copying of the material, a licence must be obtained from Access Copyright before proceeding.

Library and Archives Canada Cataloguing in Publication
Title: Attic rain : poems / by Samantha Jones.
Names: Jones, Samantha (Poet), author.
Series: Crow said poetry.
Description: Series statement: Crow said poetry
Identifiers: Canadiana (print) 20230585973 | Canadiana (ebook) 20230585981 | ISBN 9781774390986
 (softcover) | ISBN 9781774390993 (EPUB)
Subjects: LCGFT: Poetry.
Classification: LCC PS8619.O53386 A93 2024 | DDC C811/.6—dc23

Editor for the Press: Jennifer Bowering Delisle
Cover Design: Brnesh Berhe
Interior Design: Meredith Thompson
Author Photo: Silver Sabre Media Group

NeWest Press prohibits the use of *Attic Rain* in connection with the development of any software program, including, without limitation, training a machine learning or generative artificial intelligence (AI) system.

NeWest Press wishes to acknowledge that the land on which we operate is Treaty 6 territory and a traditional meeting ground and home for many Indigenous Peoples, including Cree, Saulteaux, Niitsitapi (Blackfoot), Métis, Dene, and Nakota Sioux since time immemorial. ||

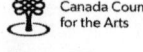 

NeWest Press acknowledges the support of the Canada Council for the Arts, the Government of Alberta through the Ministry of Arts, Culture and Status of Women , and the Edmonton Arts Council for support of our publishing program. This project is funded in part by the Government of Canada.

201, 8540–109 Street
Edmonton, Alberta T6G 1E6
780.432.9427
www.newestpress.com

No bison were harmed in the making of this book.

Printed and bound in Canada.

*for Edna*

DEAR READER,

Thank you for choosing to spend time with *Attic Rain*. This collection contains autobiographical works that explore obsessive-compulsive disorder (OCD) based on my lived experience. The scenarios and content in the poems and illustrations reflect one perspective on navigating time and space through an OCD lens. Each person living with OCD will have their own unique experiences and I cannot speak on behalf of the entire community. I have written these poems from the heart and have strived to be honest and authentic in every part of this work. Please know that these poems are not intended to be taken as advice. My aim is to share my vantage point and build compassion and awareness. I hope that you find something that resonates long after you finish reading.

Sincerely,

SAM

# Experiences

**SELF-TALK**

| | |
|---|---|
| She's Such a Perfectionist | 1 |
| Another Butterfly | 2 |
| Home Sweet Home | 3 |
| Dominoes | 4 |
| Checking the Perimeter | 5 |
| Identity Protection | 6 |
| AN ALARM IS BEEPING SOMEWHERE IN THE HOUSE | 7 |
| On Time | 8 |
| Render Unusable | 9 |
| OCD Haiku | 10 |
| Botulism Villanelle | 11 |
| Common Booby Traps | 12 |
| Index of Taking Forever | 13 |
| $R^2$ | 14 |
| Home Bitter Home | 18 |
| Floor Plans | 19 |
| OCD Mondo I | 20 |
| Attic Rain | 21 |

**INCANTATIONS**

| | |
|---|---|
| Kitchen Song | 27 |
| Door Song | 28 |
| Travel Song | 29 |
| Pet-Sitting Song | 30 |
| Bathroom Fixture Song | 31 |
| Garage Song | 32 |
| Office Song | 33 |
| Café Song | 34 |
| Goodnight Song | 35 |
| Incantations | 36 |

**TERRIBLE TOUR GUIDE**

| | |
|---|---|
| Electric Heat | 41 |
| Origin Story | 42 |
| Inseparable | 43 |
| Waiting for the School Bus | 44 |
| Walking Back to Double Check | 45 |
| OCD Mondo II | 47 |
| Flood | 48 |
| Ever Since the Flood | 49 |
| Every Day I Draw Worry Maps | 50 |
| Twister | 51 |
| Something, Something the Tip of the Iceberg | 52 |
| Polynya | 53 |
| OCD Imayo | 54 |
| Photo Stream | 55 |
| Preparing for Vacation | 56 |
| How to Leave Home Three Times at Once | 57 |
| How to Leave Home Three Times at Once (Refrain) | 58 |
| Stop Saying You're "OCD About It" | 59 |
| Was the Dog Sitting on the Sofa When I Left? | 60 |
| OCD Mondo III | 61 |
| In the Parkade | 62 |

**IN THE WORKPLACE**

| | |
|---|---|
| This Posting Will Remain Open Until Filled | 67 |
| Always Add Acid to Water | 68 |
| Shared Office | 69 |
| Shared Office (Refrain) | 70 |
| At the Office | 71 |
| Collaborations | 72 |
| The Lab Doors | 73 |
| The Lab Doors (Refrain) | 74 |
| Shutdown Procedure | 75 |
| All of My Unfinished Darlings | 76 |
| Decision Making (A How-to) | 77 |
| Am I "High-Functioning?" | 78 |

**NOTES**

**ACKNOWLEDGEMENTS**

# Self-Talk

*I'M OKAY THE WAY I AM.*

## She's Such a Perfectionist

Notebooks look best when they're empty,
second best when the used pages all look like replicas,
even though that means,
at the end, I'm still the same person
as when I started.

Crayons look best when they're brand new,
tips perfectly shaped, untouched by pressure,
lined up, light thrown through a prism,
the metallic ones spliced onto one end,
a sparkling appendix.

Small appliances look best when they're surrounded by a moat of air.

Some things slip through:
laundry piles, junk drawers, tabletops, stacks of bills—
household supernovae that run away with themselves.

## Another Butterfly

Your request lands
on my consciousness,
tissue wings dusted in pleases and
    thank-yous.

My mistake for standing so still.

This unexpected diversion
accosting attention

    I'm flustered   forced
                    afraid
to say no

thinking
    a loud chatter
thinking
    an overcrowded room
thinking
    a symphony    of banging pipes.

This might be the milligram that topples me.

# Home Sweet Home

# Dominoes

        Turn off the *stove* at least an hour before I go out
take everything *off* the top of the *stove*
    turn *off* and *unplug* the coffee maker
       *unplug* the *toaster*
         move the *toaster* away from the drying *dishes*
    make sure the *faucet* handle won't get nudged if any *dishes* shift
  check for *dripping faucets*
   listen for *dripping noises* or flowing water
  investigate any *new noises*
    check on *new appliances*
   don't *leave* with *appliances* on, except the refrigerator
it's okay to *leave* the stereo and *lamps* plugged in for the day
       *turn off* the *lamps*
       *turn off* all of the *lights*
        *check* the pilot *light*
  don't leave bills or *cheques lying* around
    make sure that the *dog* is *lying* on the sofa, not still in the yard
   double check that the *dog* is back *inside*, with water and food
    *lock* the patio door from the *inside*
    *lock* the front entrance if I manage to leave.

# Checking the Perimeter

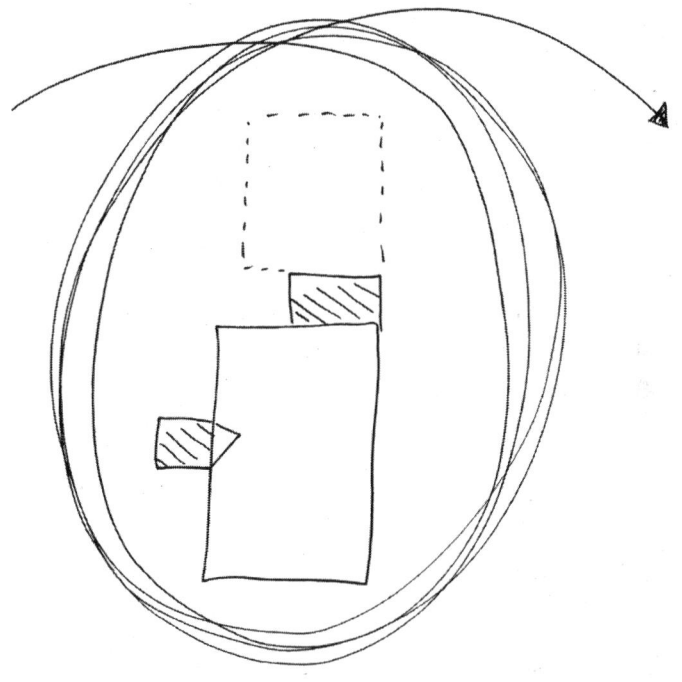

# Identity Protection

Soak a pile of receipts
in the sink.
   Lift and bleed
shopping habits
from this pulpy
beaver lodge
sitting on stainless steel
and shedding paper curds
down the drain and
        into the trap.

Or dissect each slip
along its prime meridian
then its equator.
   Cleave it
into tiny continents
throw away half
this garbage day.

# AN ALARM IS BEEPING SOMEWHERE IN THE HOUSE

MY HAIR JUMPS OFF MY SKIN. MY SKIN PUCKERS

AROUND EACH STRAND. JAMMING THE HAIRS IN THEIR

TINY DOORS. SEALING UP MY OUTER LAYER. MY HANDS

QUIVER. BLOOD PLAYS MY EARDRUMS, PEDAL ON THE
BASS. ARTERIAL WATERFALL. I HEAR THE WHIRLPOOL.

QUICKLY. I ENTER AND EXIT ITS PROJECTION. DOPPLER.
I MOVE AROUND THE HOUSE, CHASING THE CHANGE IN

FREQUENCY. WARMER WARMER COLDER WARMER
COLDER COLDER WARMER HOT HOT HOTTER. I DON'T
KNOW THE DEVICES BY EAR. IT'S TOO UNPLEASANT TO

TEST THEM. I HAVE NO BASIS FOR COMPARISON. I SWEAT.
MY HUSBAND DOES THE TESTING WHEN I'M NOT AROUND.
I CHECK THE ONLINE MANUAL. WHAT MODEL DO I HAVE?

WHAT DO FOUR LONG BEEPS AND A PAUSE MEAN?
WHAT DOES A BLINKING ORANGE LIGHT MEAN? NO. NOT
THREE QUICK BEEPS. FOUR LONG BEEPS. AM I GOING
TO DIE? WHO WILL FIND ME? WILL THEY DIE TOO? TAKE
OUT THE BATTERIES SO I CAN THINK. TAKE OUT THE
BATTERIES. CONCENTRATE. I'M TRYING TO THINK.
SOMEONE TAKE OUT THE BATTERIES. THE BATTERIES.

# On Time

How do you live someone else's timeline?

How do you measure adequate time?

Is productivity asymptotic?

How does one brain divide and conquer?

How do you define urgency?

Did you move on or move over?

# Render Unusable

Build an accidental fort
of old car seats,
change pads, stroller parts,
all the cushy bits.

My fear of strangers
retrieving and reusing
unfit items clogs
a common space.

They'll multiply
into a precarious scarp,
until the garage is full,
and the pile of manuals
can no longer support itself,

> slides
>> off the edge
>> of the shelf.

What if I wait
until everyone's sleeping
and melt them down myself?

## OCD Haiku

river swells with melt
think about raising items
two feet off the floor


hot afternoons seed
cumulus clouds and anvils
compromise the roof


first night cold enough
for the furnace to kick in
dreams of pilot lights


deep-freeze encroaches
walls with vapour barriers
pray the pipes hold strong

## Botulism Villanelle

Thumbs trace circles on aluminum cans
stopping to linger on each accrued dent
dispelling worries of my buying hands

weekly ritual, detailed grocery scans
perusing for lids peaked up in small tents
thumbs trace circles on aluminum cans

careful attention to product lifespans
mindful shopping a relief from torment
dispelling worries of my buying hands

pantry abundant with weeks of meal plans
outcomes differ from well-meaning intent
thumbs trace circles on aluminum cans

inspecting dropped food as soon as it lands
disposing items disfigured or bent
dispelling worries of my buying hands

double check before pouring into pans
persistent, consistent need to prevent
thumbs trace circles on aluminum cans
dispelling worries of my buying hands.

# Common Booby Traps

Look,
    *The outdoor faucet could freeze in a cold snap, rupture, and leak into the walls.*

blink, and again,
    *A storm water drain passes through the same wall as the outdoor faucet pipes.*

billions of little loops
    *Cold weather condensation could pool on panes and make the paint peel.*

where neurons should be—
    *Attic rain could infiltrate, percolate, and bloom across bedroom ceilings.*

right now is not a good time,
    *Did you know that old popcorn ceilings may contain asbestos?*

but is it ever ideal to be stranded
    *I'm worried about radon, not asbestos. I heard that radon is a silent killer.*

in your own catastrophe?
    *The highest concentration of appliances is in the kitchen.*

For me, the wave wanes
    *The crock full of ladles could tip over and knock a stovetop knob on.*

but every occurrence
    *The almost empty pot could boil dry, burn, and set off the smoke detector.*

leaves its shadow,
    *Dust could make the smoke and carbon monoxide detector malfunction.*

is the basement
    *And then there's the sitting around, waiting for a replacement to arrive.*

for next time.

# Index of Taking Forever

archache
annotime
belabourables
concight
descrush
evidend
forender
gradire
handunder
infomerit
jumbless
kredentry
leveledge
milestressed
multitire
nullitude
openscarce
ordefy
proofdream
quitrap
replimp
roarganize
secursed
sensitry
trushed
untrushed
valover
weekdance
ximple
yourstunt
zippried

$R^2$

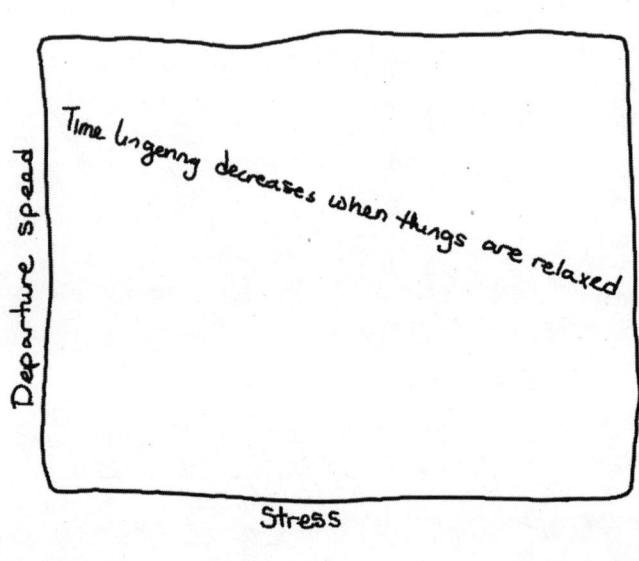

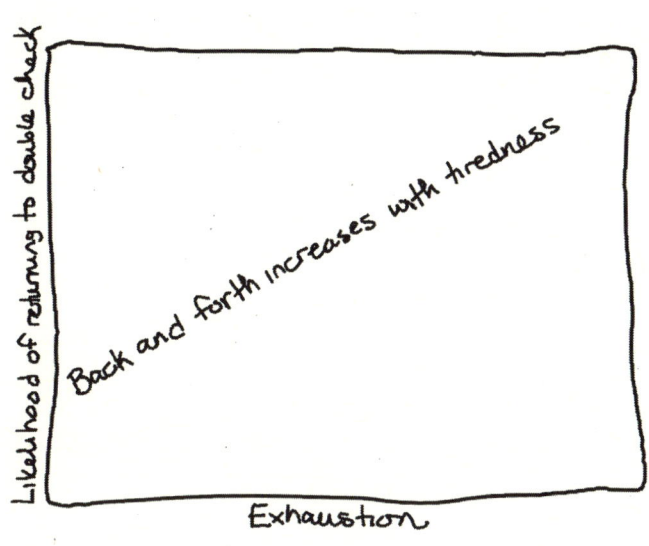

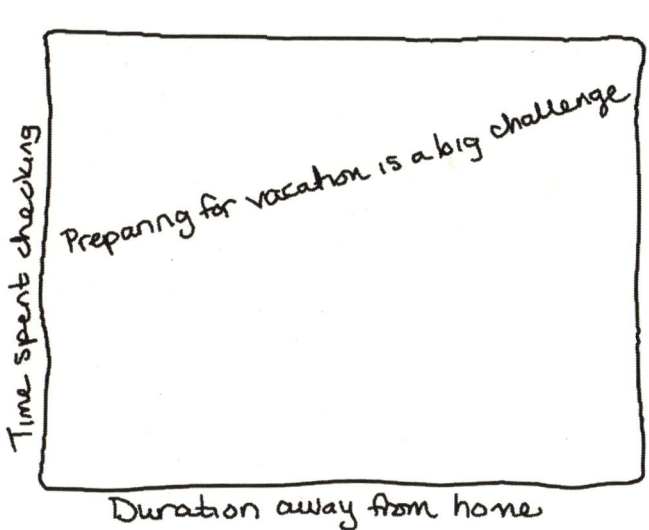

# Home Bitter Home

Once I have settled
for the day, night, weekend
it's easy to keep an eye
on things

on a path forward
free from fog
tuned to connections,
that turn on and off

    I end up with an iron
    that sits in its box for years
    before I give in and loan it
    to house guests

who don't know
the way that things must sit
on their own,
disconnected disarmed

the code of conduct
surrounded by a nothingness
empty space
that fire can't jump

    I skip the home listings
    with gas ranges, kitchens
    to visit again and again,
    the worry would smother me.

Floor Plans

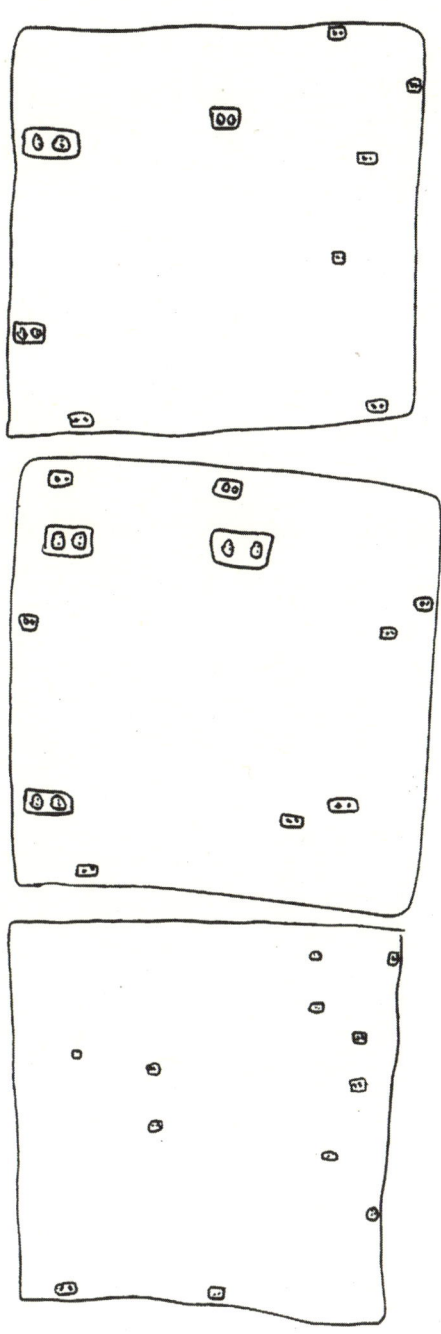

# OCD Mondo I

Futures for window chips? Frost coaxes spiderwebs.

## Attic Rain

Thoughts rise on warm air and wrap
the rafters, beams embraced by

crystals, a closing hollow, one delicate layer
over another, deposits lining the inside

of an icebox, the threat of melt is
always present, and on the day

I least expect it, this
deep-freeze will
end and
it will
all come
pouring
down.

# Incantations

*And then I realized I was making music.*

# Kitchen Song

Off off off off
off ≀ off ≀

        off off off off
        off ≀ off ≀
        off off off off
        off ≀ off ≀

off off off off
off ≀ off ≀
good

unplugged unplugged
unplugged unplugged

everything good.

## Door Song

𝄢 locked locked locked locked
locked locked locked locked 𝄂

# Travel Song

passport wallet keys phone
passport wallet keys phone
passport wallet keys phone
passport wallet keys phone

(General Pause)

# Pet-Sitting Song

food water in in
food water in
food water in in
food water in

off ？ off ？
off ？ off ？

# Bathroom Fixture Song

Off off off ⸮
Off off off ⸮

nothing ⸮ nothing ⸮
nothing ⸮ nothing ⸮

(increase repetition with tempo)

## Garage Song

shut shut shut shut
shut shut shut ⸮
shut shut shut shut
shut shut shut ⸮

## Office Song

Locked locked
    locked locked

unplugged? unplugged?

shut shut
    shut shut
shut shut
    shut shut

keys card wallet phone.

# Café Song

Nothing
nothing ₹ nothing ₹
nothing

got everything.

(look back while walking away)

## Goodnight Song

Locked locked lock—ed
Locked locked lock—ed
Locked locked lock—ed
Locked locked lock—ed

Locked      Locked

off off off off

Off         Off

unplugged unplugged unplugged unplugged

off

locked locked alarm.

# Incantations

Patterns that make
wonder,
my secret songs
of beats and breaths,
a tour guide chartered
for my whole life,
sight-seeing at home,
visits to all top ten distractions—
look here look there look here AGAIN
Again, again
a loop de loop, REPEAT
Repeat
repeat.

# TERRIBLE TOUR GUIDE

*Yes, I would say I'm detail oriented.*

# Electric Heat

# Origin Story

In the beginning
I was just a girl
who liked the pristine—
crayons arranged ROYGBIV,
factory settings, and stickers
still on white backing.

Perfectly planned notebooks,
categorized knickknacks,
and sentiments tucked away,
not yet ready for garbage day.

I learned how to lock up
and use dull knives,
put my own spin
on family traditions,
the art of list making
on take-out menus,
    flyers,
    sticky notes,
    envelopes,
    whatever I've got.

My magic expanded
to fill a growing shell,
threading every cell
with a string of worries, pearls
too tight to slip off over my head
and return to their music box.

# Inseparable

Dear co-conspirator,

I want you to know that I have stopped
trying to expel you.

Can you even survive outside the body?

Naked and soft,
tossed aside—

I didn't think so.

You are a thing to manage,
inoperable.

The warp on this loom,
the rest of my life woven
around you.

# Waiting for the School Bus

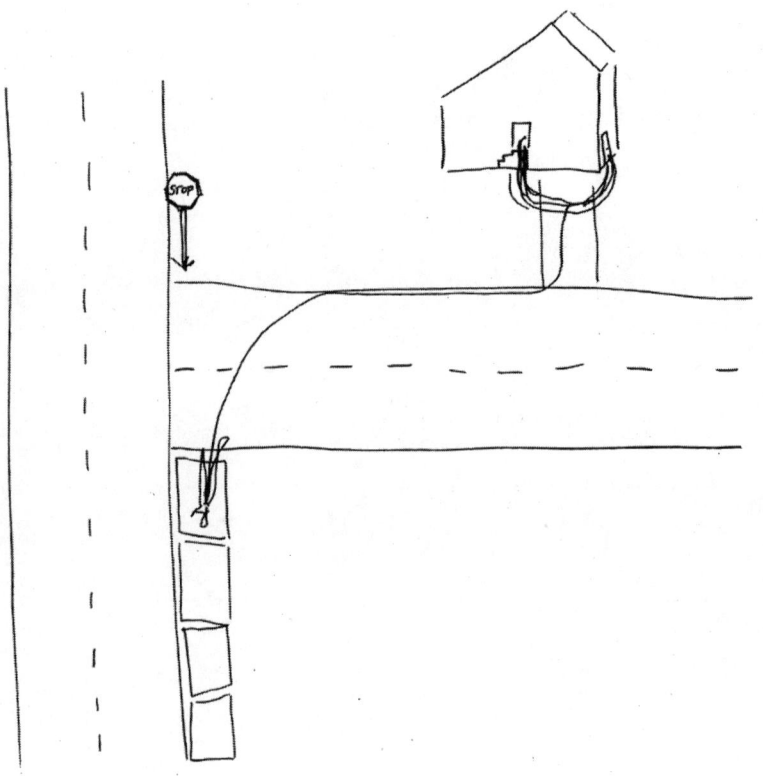

## Walking Back to Double Check

I draw worry maps

with invisible ink

on carpet tiles      maple planks

my feet,

accomplices to assorted rituals,

sometimes sparked by nothing at all.

Pure action.

The day is made of many trails

    back

  and

    forth

until I'm certain

I'm capable of leaving      well enough alone.

I've made a life of treading

lightly,

the entrance and exit

to this maze

        undetectable

by most—

until overlapping footprints

        up and down and up and down and up and down my front steps

and into the snow

give me away.

# OCD Mondo II

Why does the rain pool? Grass ceded to cement siren song.

# Flood

Pile another one on
my aching mind—
      cause and effect
            cause and effect—
a scaffold of strain
bowed once again
to accommodate this new
      obsession.

I stand on my front porch
and watch the river swell.

# Ever Since the Flood

## Every Day I Draw Worry Maps

This body moves
according to its own method,
reverberating, retuning, repeating,
choosing soothing routes through space,
each place requires careful
consideration.

These feet sketch memories,
paths worn over and over,
a part of me left pressed
into the earth.

To retrace my steps,
just follow the web
of shallow rivulets.

# Twister

That drumbeat,
my baseline,
loud wind chime,
when the skies turned green—

a heart pound that could bury me
under a silo, blown apart metal sheets,
the romance of getting into the centre—

wind whips, wails    stops
to catch a breath before

dragging me through the other side:
curious, terrified.

# Something, Something the Tip of the Iceberg

Worries calving into home
and work and everywhere in between
    underwater  under pressure    undercutting      until
I tumble and collapse into the sea.

A wave sucks me down
    into a frigid pool,

but I am ice.

I push back to the surface,
My apex bobs up over and over
and punctures the slick skin
between the sea and sky.

# Polynya

I am an ice factory
building tiny rafts
sending them into the wind.

I am stubborn open water
pulling away scabs
quickly replaced by newer,
thinner ones.

## OCD Imayo

For some it's entertainment; locked doors as playthings,
puzzles, peppered clues, a feat; Friday team building.
For me, conjure a locked room; good night's sleep, mind rest,
A secure capsule, blank slate; to draw the next day.

## Photo Stream

You took photos
of the room before you left
so later you wouldn't need
to travel across town.

We walk because
we're compelled,
under the midnight sun,
we walk because we can.

I sometimes do that too—
you relaxed, I was also fluent
in self-doubt, disbelief,
distrust in my own
ability to flick a switch

and remember     the mind
plays tricks           on all of us.

# Preparing for Vacation

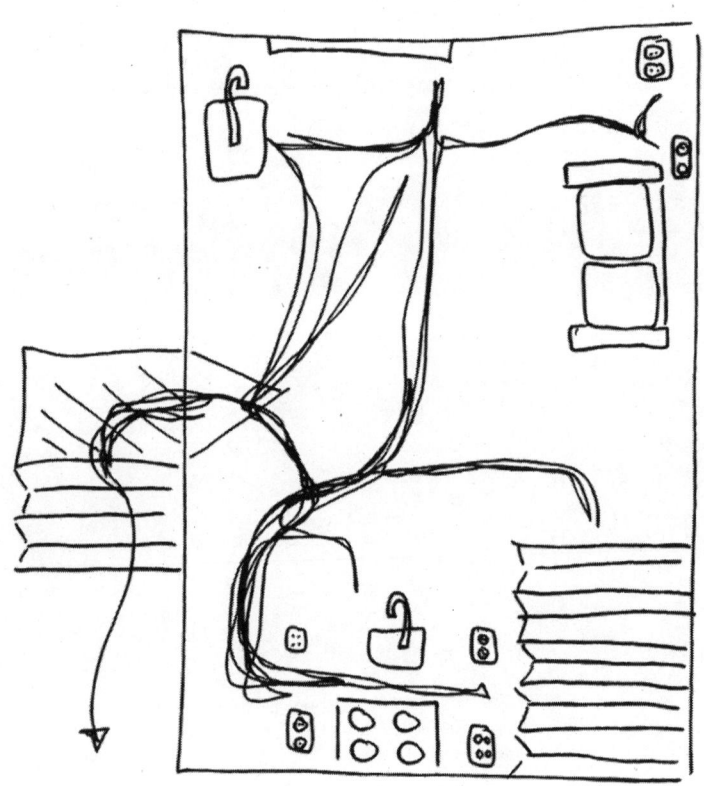

# How to Leave Home Three Times at Once

I belong to
a special order

I belong to
a complicated exit
that ebbs
and flows back through
the door and up
the stairs
to start again and leave the same
way as before.

Have you felt
the way the brain can
grip skin to metal
fingers flash frozen
on the handle
that needed to be grabbed
one more time
two more times
to triple check
I let go
my shriveled skin
tugs and releases
with a pop.

I step down
one two three
onto the walk
and back up again
back down again
back up again
hand outstretched
just to be sure.

# How to Leave Home Three Times at Once (Refrain)

I belong to
a special order

~~I break again~~ in and leave the same
~~way I came~~ exit
~~that flbls~~ back through
Have you felt
the way the brain can
grip skin to metal
~~things elastic~~ frozen
~~to a slack veiled~~ skin
~~clings molecules be~~ grabbed
with a pop.

~~Just pour sure.~~
~~hand out~~ stretched
~~back the way again~~

## Stop Saying You're "OCD About It"

This manifesto
could write itself
if I asked you about:

hands washed raw, locks worn down,
cords yanked thin, plug prongs dulled,
cloth threadbare, food thrown out,
work redone, sleepless nights,
wounds unhealed.

## Was the Dog Sitting on the Sofa When I Left?

Now I need to start again
to peek at her
open the door
walk by my own footprints
drive back to the house
turn around.

Turn around
drive back to the house
walk by my own footprints
open the door
to peek at her
now I need to start again.

# OCD Mondo III

Who warps the fence? Saturated soil's slow nudge.

# In the Parkade

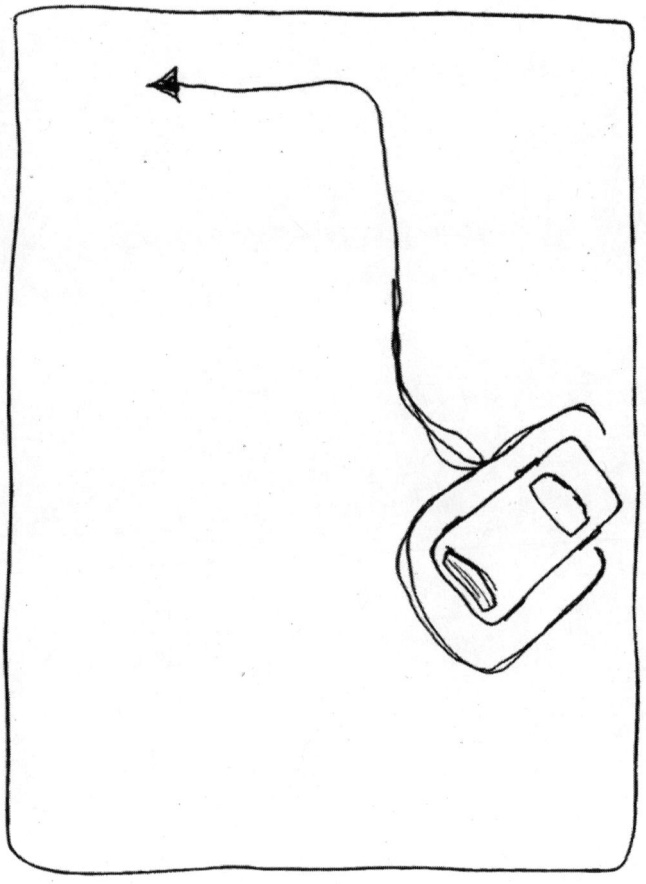

# In the Workplace

*It's fast-paced, challenging, and always changing.*

# This Posting Will Remain Open Until Filled

Flexible, disciplined,
proactive, reactive,
spontaneous, well-planned,
organized, but effortless,
in control, but never a control freak.

Adept at adjusting—evolving,
tracking moving targets,
proficient in uncertainty,
always put together, whimsical,
but not too whimsical.

# Always Add Acid to Water

The dilution needs to be   s l o w

one
drip
at
a
time,
gloved hands hold
glass flasks
inside a fume hood,
don't let the negative pressure
steal the rhythm of your breath.

Even as I write this,
I double check so I don't mislead you
into exothermic reaction.

## Shared Office

I know you are still working
so I pause	before walking back,
I'll pretend I forgot something
	or maybe I'll shrug and say,
the kettle was acting up today.

The trip back is quick
but you will hear me
boots on floor
hand on doorknob
I hope you have your headphones on.

# Shared Office (Refrain)

I know you have your headphones on.
...doorknob before walking back,
...forgot something
but you will... I'll shrug and say,
... up today.

# At the Office

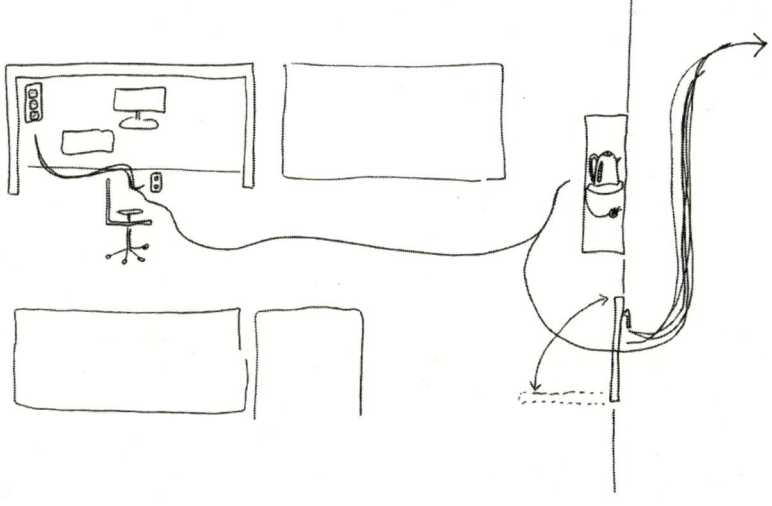

# Collaborations

Fists clenched around
unripe deliverables
too green to be peeled
from my fingers and
released into the basket.
I block the critical path.

I long to be reliable,
the go-to person,
minus the burden
of being certain.

I'll sound my own siren,
come rushing in calling out:
please doubt me
all the way back
to the drawing board.

# The Lab Doors

It's after hours
and I'm the last to leave.
I shut down the instruments,
tidy up, wash my hands,
step into the hallway,
and pull the door shut behind me,
look to the black dome mounted
on the ceiling. Is anyone watching?

The lab has two exits
and I have to check both,
back
and forth
back
and forth,
then step back to survey
my work, try to find the big picture.

# The Lab Doors (Refrain)

It's after hours
and I'm the last to leave.
I shut down the instruments,
tidy up, wash my hands,
step into the hallway,
and pull the door shut behind me,
look to the black dome mounted
on the ceiling. Is anyone watching?

The lab has two exits
~~backtrack~~ I draw to check both,
then step back to survey
my work, try to find the big picture.

# Shutdown Procedure

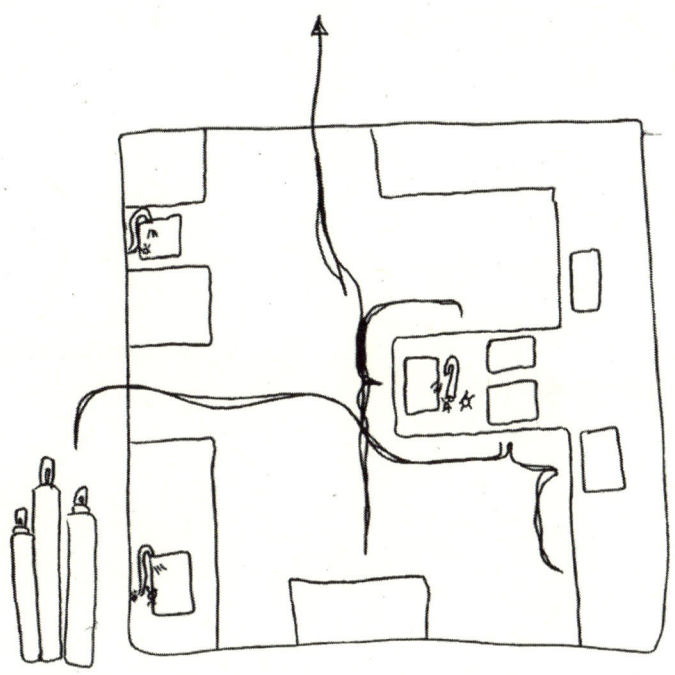

# All of My Unfinished Darlings

I return again and again
to dig for errors, omissions
an ongoing excavation
that flips progress
inside out. I promise
to just fix the hem
but leave the stiches loose,
a flap half-dangling
held up with a safety pin

## Decision Making (A How-to)

1. Ask a bunch of people what they think you should do.

2. Listen to them. Each tells you something different.

3. Go home and have a nap.

4.

5.

# Am I "High-Functioning?"

Did you think I was difficult
                particular
                  controlling?

My motivations aren't malicious
many more mornings
may start with lists and logs
of things double-checked
it's nothing personal
      I hide it from     most everyone,

which it isn't very hard to do
when outcome is preferred to process
in a world focused on what you make
not how many back-and-forths
it takes to get there.

I don't want to be remembered
for my productivity.

Can I leave things like this?

                Without being cured?

# Notes

### AN ALARM IS BEEPING SOMEWHERE IN THE HOUSE

Some style elements in "AN ALARM IS BEEPING SOMEWHERE IN THE HOUSE" are after Billy-Ray Belcourt (2019), "I DOUCHE WHILE KESHA'S 'PRAYING' PLAYS FROM MY IPHONE ON REPEAT", *NDN Coping Mechanisms,* Canada: House of Anansi Press Inc., 112 pp.

### OCD Haiku

This four-haiku series was created considering the guidelines suggested in Terry Ann Carter (2014), *Hue: A Day at Butchart Gardens - a Haiku Primer.* British Columbia, Canada: Leaf Press, 52 pp.

### Floor Plans

This piece reimagines the home by redefining the criteria used to map interior spaces; it allows the familiarity of a place to be driven by an OCD perspective. This reorientation prioritizes the interactions between me and the structure over architectural accuracy. To create "Floor Plans," I mapped electrical outlets from memory based on checking routines. The outlet icon sizes represent the perceived risk; so larger icons receive more scrutiny during my daily life. This OCD cartography strips away the other components of the house and emphasizes a distribution of features through an OCD lens. It pinpoints areas of concentrated discomfort and contrasts these locations with parts of the home that are avoided or even forgotten. As a map, "Floor Plans" is unique to me, and co-exists as an alternate framework for a space that is shared with and lived in by others.

## OCD Mondo I, OCD Mondo II, and OCD Mondo III

The resource "Mondo: Poetic Forms" by Robert Lee Brewer published online on February 27, 2017, by *Writer's Digest* was used as inspiration for these poems. The dialogue between intrusive questions and foreboding answers is a variation on the collaborative tradition of the Mondo form.

### Incantations

The poems in this section are specific to time, place, and context. Each routine is dependent on the items that I perceive as hazards, the arrangement of these items, and the influence of recent events or general wellness and stress levels. I reviewed the routines in my home while documenting them. I said them aloud to capture the repetition and pauses as accurately as possible. I acted them out with the movements that accompany the checking. In paying such close attention, I kept asking myself what I was sacrificing to put this on paper and if I was interfering by focusing on the patterns as I executed the routines. To recall and record an authentic transcription of each incantation, I selected the most persistent routines that engaged muscle memory and recall. By the time this book is in your hands, these compulsion songs will have changed. In this way, this section is a time capsule.

### Twister

A nod to the best natural disaster movie, of course. But also, an exploration of how appreciation and intense interest can be loci of intrusive thoughts.

### Polynya

A polynya is an area of open water in ocean regions otherwise covered in sea ice.

### OCD Imayo

The resource "Imayo: Poetic Forms" by Robert Lee Brewer published online on February 8, 2019, by *Writer's Digest* was used as inspiration for this poem.

### Three pairs of poems and their refrains

The poems "How to Leave Home Three Times at Once," "Shared Office," and "The Lab Doors" are paired with refrain versions that feature overwritten lines of the same text. The form of the refrain versions mimics the back-and-forth in the routines described in each narrative. When the direction of movement changes in the narrative, the flow direction of subsequent lines changes, from top to bottom of the page to bottom to top, for example. These flow direction changes may happen once or multiple times in a single poem. Overwriting may result in the execution of the compulsions becoming the focus while obscuring the big picture, or in the case of "The Lab Doors," the back-and-forth may collapse onto itself and become an almost hidden struggle.

### Collaborations

For all the people waiting for me.

### Am I "High-functioning?"

The term high-functioning is sometimes used to describe people with neurodivergences or mental illnesses. It is often considered offensive or ableist, particularly when referring to autism spectrum disorder. In this concluding poem, I reclaim the term, which I believe is too casually used in mainstream media and discourse. I use it satirically and as an act of resistance. The final line, "Without being cured?" is not synonymous with an absence of treatment or support.

# Acknowledgements

Like the rest of this book and the experiences that inspired each poem, writing these acknowledgements can't be separated from my OCD. Perhaps this is the section that scares me the most—what if I forget something or someone? I worry that an omission might become a haunting. I love reading acknowledgements in books. I often read them first and look to them to appreciate a writer's journey, their community, and all of their loves.

I want to start by thanking my late grandmother, Edna, to whom this book is dedicated. If I could talk to you today, I would tell you that I see you, I understand some of the challenges you faced, and I will continue to tell my OCD story for myself, but also for all the people who don't get that chance. I love you.

Thank you to my family and friends including special shout-outs to SJ, Sharon, and Kristina, who always read and discuss my work with care. Thank you to my son Theo for the imaginative energy and love you bring into my life every day, and for your excellent advice that if I want to be an author, I need to write a book and then tell people about it. Thank you to Ryan for sharing this creative journey and to my parents for encouraging me to be whimsical. Thank you, Alexa G., Alexa R., Araleigh, Candice, Charlie, Chris B., Chris C., Jessie, Joyce, Kirti, Kristina B., Megan, Moni, Patrick, Samantha, Tolu, Uche, Wakefield, and Zoe for pumping me up and being community. Thank you, Eric, Tola, and Silvana, for making me look rad in my author photo.

I have a deep appreciation for all the instructors, mentors, and peers that I worked with and learned from during the Creative Writing Certificate Program at the University of Calgary, especially Diane Guichon, Vivian Hansen, and Judith Williams who believed in my ideas, encouraged me, and made room for my voice. Thank you to the Alexandra Writers' Centre Society (AWCS), the Espresso Poetry and Poetry Café folks, Lisa Murphy Lamb and Loft 112, the Iceland Writers Retreat, and angela rawlings and MOONLINE Writers' Lab. A sense of community and a space to experiment and grow as a creative goes a long way. The Diverse Voices Roundtable, the Banff Centre Spring Writers Retreat 2021 cohort and faculty, the League of Canadian Poets (LCP) Parenting Poets committee, and the Festival of Literary Diversity (FOLD) have been great sources of connection and creative exchange during the period I worked on this project.

Several of the poems in this collection germinated from writing prompts during Poetry Café (spearheaded by Laurie Fuhr) and several others were workshopped with the Espresso Poetry group. Thank you to Judith Pond for your thoughtful feedback on parts of this manuscript, to Teresa Wong for your encouragement regarding my OCD sketches/visual poems, and to the editors and anonymous reviewers who provided feedback during the querying process.

Thank you to the editors, journals, and organizations who published versions of poems included in this collection. "Identity Protection" in *Parentheses Journal*; "AN ALARM IS BEEPING SOMEWHERE IN THE HOUSE" previously published as "ALARM" in *The Capilano Review*; "OCD Haiku" in the 2021 Festival of Literary Diversity program *Voices From the FOLD: A Festival Magazine, Year Six*; "Kitchen Song," "Door Song," "Travel Song," "Garage Song," "Incantations," and the image "Home Sweet Home" in *Blanket Sea*; "Twister" in the LCP *Fresh Voices* and the LCP *Poetry Pause*; and "How to Leave Home Three Times at Once" in the LCP chapbook anthology *You are a Flower Growing off the Side of a Cliff*, edited by Rayanne Haines.

There are many folks who consistently uplift and treat my OCD poetry with care. Thank you to the LCP for the invitation to read at the inaugural session of the Cross-Pollinations Virtual Health Humanities Series. Sharing my OCD work and the discussions that followed reinforced that there was a need for more OCD-centred perspectives in literature. I am indebted to Sarah de Leeuw and Kyle Flemmer and the Blasted Tree for their extraordinary support of my work, and to Drew McEwan and Olajide Salawu for engaging with and writing about my OCD poetry with so much care. What a gift!

Thank you to Chelene Knight for insightful and sensitive coaching and Dr. Jenna Butler for your mentorship and support as I establish myself as a voice in Canadian Literature. A massive thank you to my editor, Jen Bowering Delisle for your careful readings, thoughtful discussions, and kind approach to bringing a book into the world. The team at NeWest Press has been an incredible source of support to get this project across the finish line. I couldn't have done it without you.

Finally, I am grateful to you for spending time with *Attic Rain*.

Samantha Jones (she/her) is a writer, copyeditor, and earth scientist based in Moh'kins'tsis (Calgary, Alberta) on the traditional territory of Treaty 7 peoples and the home of Métis Nation of Alberta, Districts 5 and 6. She is a magazine and journal enthusiast with work published in *Room*, *CV2*, *Grain*, *THIS*, *GeoHumanities*, *Arctic*, *EVENT*, *The Capilano Review*, and elsewhere. Her visual OCD poetry chapbook, *Site Orientation*, was published by the Blasted Tree in 2022. Sam is proud of her mixed heritage, which is Black Canadian and white settler. *Attic Rain* is her first full-length poetry collection and perhaps most importantly, blue whales are her favourite candy.

In 2017, to honour NeWest Press' 40th anniversary, we inaugurated a new poetry series to go alongside our Nunatak First Fiction, Prairie Play, and Writer as Critic series: Crow Said Poetry. Crow Said is named in honour of Robert Kroetsch's foundational 1977 novel *What The Crow Said*. The series aims to shed light on places and people outside of the literary mainstream. It is our intention that the poets featured in this series will continue Robert Kroetsch's literary tradition of innovation, interrogation, and generosity of spirit.

*Tar Swan* — David Martin
*That Light Feeling Under Your Feet* — Kayla Geitzler
*Paper Caskets* — Emilia Danielewska
*let us not think of them as barbarians* — Peter Midgley
*Lullabies in the Real World* — Meredith Quartermain
*The Response of Weeds: A Misplacement of Black Poetry on the Prairies* — Bertrand Bickersteth
*Coconut* — Nisha Patel
*rump + flank* — Carol Harvey Steski
*How to Hold a Pebble* — Jaspreet Singh
*Kink Bands* — David Martin
*Attic Rain* — Samantha Jones
*Dreams of the Epoch & the Rock* — Jaspreet Singh

This collection has been typeset in Fanwood.